LIANA DANSER MORGAN

180 Degree Fairy Tale

Copyright © 2025 by Liana Danser Morgan

All rights reserved. No part of this publication may be reproduced, stored or transmitted in any form or by any means, electronic, mechanical, photocopying, recording, scanning, or otherwise without written permission from the publisher. It is illegal to copy this book, post it to a website, or distribute it by any other means without permission.

First edition

This book was professionally typeset on Reedsy.
Find out more at reedsy.com

Dedication

*My book is dedicated to my Mother Lucille and my Father Gordon,
Along with my Daughter Brooke and my Son Donnie
I love all of you very much!*

Think more than you say, and notice everything

Contents

Introduction	1
1 The Forgotten Call	3
2 Only in Vegas, The Business of Reinvention	5
3 Exclusivity	7
4 Stepping Into a Fairy Tale	11
5 A Hidden Gem	14
6 Unpacking the Future	17
7 The Tenant with Benefits	20
8 Under the Radar, Over the Moon	24
9 Unspoken Promises	27
10 Illusion of Abundance	31
11 Curiosity Killed the Trust	34
12 The Noise in His Silence	39
13 A Soul's Quiet Escape	44
14 No Fairy Tale Ending Here	51
15 Back to the Beginning Again	55
16 The Energy That Shapes Our Lives	61
17 Understanding Soul Energetic System	63
18 Protecting Your Light Energy (High Vibration)	69
19 My Vision for the World	74
20 Conclusion	77
Epilogue	79
Afterword	80

Introduction

In my memoir, I will take readers on a journey through a pivotal period of my life that led me to discover that I am a super empath. A super empath is someone with an extraordinary capacity for empathy, emotional intelligence, and sensitivity to the emotions of others. Super empaths are often people pleasers, highly intuitive, absorb emotions deeply, possess a strong moral compass, exhibit profound compassion, and demonstrate resilience and strength. They have a heightened ability to recognize narcissistic behavior and often serve as emotional healers.

Looking back, I now understand why I experienced emotions so intensely or behaved in specific ways, particularly in large groups. It was often difficult to distinguish between my own emotions and those I absorbed from others, which led to moments of unexpected tears or sudden frustration. My heightened sensitivity shaped my experiences in ways I didn't fully comprehend at the time.

As a child, I recall walking into our living room and seeing my mother cry while watching a sad movie on TV. Without hesitation, I burst into tears. Confused, she turned to me and asked, "What's wrong with you?" As I'm a sobbing mess, I said, "You're crying." It wasn't just because I saw her sadness—I was feeling it as though it were my own.

My father is a wonderful man, and I am incredibly grateful for the stability and structure he provided in my life. However, he had a temper and maintained an almost militant level of order in our home. I remember him running his finger along the top of my bedroom door, checking for dust. "What's this?" he asked sternly. I stood frozen. I must have been around seven years old. Then, to my surprise, he smiled, hugged me, and said, "I'm just kidding, but now you know—when you get bigger, dust up there too." Whew!

—I had passed the inspection that day. These "inspections" were part of our weekday routine; weekends were our reprieve.

At times, my father would return home from work in a bad mood, and my mother would forewarn us. My sister and I would stare anxiously through our bedroom windows, watching for his Ford pickup truck. As he pulled up to the front of the house, I studied his face, his movements. The way he shifted the gear into park—if he slammed it—was an early indicator. If he shut the door hard, we knew to tread lightly. Without realizing it, I was learning to read energy, to assess the emotional climate before stepping into it. Over the years, he mellowed, but those early experiences shaped how I navigated emotions—both my own and those of others.

Growing up in this environment, where emotions were often tied to unspoken energy shifts, intensified my sensitivity and ultimately shaped my identity as a super empath.

As I grew older, I've become better equipped, distinguishing my own emotions from those I absorbed and shielding myself from negative energy. My awareness has only strengthened, allowing me to sense the energy of a room or detect the emotional state of someone the moment they walk through the door. At times, I can even feel when someone carries another energy attached to them—a concept I will explore further in my memoir.

While all empaths feel deeply, super empaths often exhibit stronger boundaries, a heightened sense of self, and the ability to transform their emotional awareness into action. We can detect deception, resist manipulation, and, in some cases, mirror a narcissist's tendencies back at them, effectively standing up to their toxic behavior. This, I later realized, became a pivotal strength in my relationship with Edward.

Recognizing my super empath nature has been both a burden and a gift. It made me susceptible to manipulation but also gave me the power to see through it. Now, I embrace it as a source of strength, using it to protect myself and guide others through their own emotional landscapes.

1

The Forgotten Call

It was a Saturday afternoon sun blazed over Las Vegas, casting sharp shadows across the parking lot. I sat in my car, the engine idling, my phone still connected to Bluetooth. The conversation with Edward had just ended—or so I thought.

"I love you, baby," he had said, his voice warm and reassuring. "I miss you and I can't wait to see you in a few days!", he exclaimed. "Oh! One more thing…I probably won't call you tonight when I get home since it'll be too late. Gotta go, bye!"

I smiled with contentment. I knew this time we'd make it through any challenge going forward.

Then, before I could disconnect the call, I heard a rustling sound and voices come through the speakers.

"Hi, baby." His voice was different now—softer, eager. A faint, feminine voice responding. The sound of a car door closing as she gets into the car. Then the unmistakable sound of a kiss.

"Are you ready?" Edward asked, excitement in his voice. "It's going to be fun tonight!"

My body went rigid. I could feel my heart beating in my head, the adrenaline was racing. My mind raced to make sense of what I was hearing, but the truth was already sinking in, heavy and undeniable.

I should have hung up. I should have spared myself of what came next. But I didn't. I sat there, listening, my whole body was trembling uncontrollably.

And then, like a knife twisting in an already deep wound, I heard my own name.

"So, I'm seeing my attorney on Monday", Edward said, his voice serious with a bit of amusement. "I'll be taking her off my trust and next, I'll be working on getting her out of my house in Vegas." he said in a low calm tone. "I just know she'll destroy it, she's been abusive to me also," he had said in a convincing manner. "It has really taken a toll on me."

Never had I experienced emotions of this magnitude. Every word was a betrayal, every syllable proof that our relationship was nothing more than a lie.

For forty-five agonizing minutes, I listened. Listened as the man I loved unconditionally painted me as a mental tyrant. As he planned a future that no longer included me. As he made her believe she was the only one.

Finally, unable to take another second, I pressed the button and ended the call.

I continued to sit in my car, in a state of confusion, trying to make sense of what just occurred. It was a nightmare, a nightmare in its infancy….

2

Only in Vegas, The Business of Reinvention

Growing up in Albuquerque, New Mexico, I was blessed with a childhood marked by warmth, stability, and unwavering support. My parents, who have shared 62 years of marriage, created a home where I was encouraged to discover my own path rather than follow a prescribed plan. After high school, I pursued my studies at the University of New Mexico, earning a bachelor's degree that laid a solid foundation for my future.

My professional journey began in Las Vegas, Nevada, where I spent over two decades immersed in the structured world of corporate finance. My days were filled with spreadsheets, deadlines, and financial reports—a life of order and routine. However, following the sale of the company, I found myself at a crossroads. The prospect of returning to the rigid corporate environment, with its unyielding demands and limited freedom, no longer resonated with me. I longed for a change that would grant me greater personal autonomy.

Las Vegas has a way of making reinvention seem effortless. In a city built on spectacle and indulgence, stepping into a world of glamour and luxury felt natural. Becoming a high-end companion—an escort, a provider, or whatever one chooses to call it—wasn't something I ever envisioned for myself. It kind of fell into my lap and it made sense. I perceive it as the upgraded version of dating; both are guaranteed to walk away with something. This choice was one that granted me the freedom I craved and the financial stability I needed. I controlled my time, my plans, my destiny.

This wasn't a decision I made overnight; it was a gradual process. Before stepping into the world being a high-end companion, a friend introduced me to the owner of a lucrative webcam modeling studio in Las Vegas. Time was of the essence, and I needed money fast. My mindset was simple: Don't think, just do. There was no room to analyze, weigh the pros and cons, or, most importantly, consider the risk of my family finding out. It wasn't meant to be permanent—or so I told myself. But I took the risk. My life took a complete 180. To succeed, I had to treat it like a business, maximizing every opportunity to increase my earnings. That meant being unique, creative, and, most of all, exuding confidence. Over time, I built a lucrative base of loyal members on my website, which then escalated to meeting me in person in Las Vegas. Finally, I stood as my own boss, enjoying the freedom, control, and financial stability that I had always sought.

While some may judge the choices I've made, I recognize that my career is only one part of who I am. My identity is shaped by my experiences, the risks I have taken, and the way I treat others. My heart, my dreams, and my soul extend far beyond any single aspect of my professional life.

3

Exclusivity

It was during January 2021, and I decided I wasn't going to take on new clients. Yet when Edward called, there was something about his voice—lively, confident, almost electric. He introduced himself, shared a glimpse of his background, and briefly explained his company and its industry. He had a way of making you feel like you were the most interesting person he had ever spoken to; I could hear the excitement in his voice. Even more, he had a knack for making me laugh throughout the conversation. Despite my better judgment, I couldn't resist the promise of a fun evening with someone who had made me feel so comfortable in just ten minutes.

When I arrived at his home, he greeted me with a glass of Caymus, one of my favorite Cabernet's. The dinner he prepared was exquisite—hors d'oeuvres carefully arranged, a beautiful salad, a main course that looked straight out of a five-star restaurant. The dining table, set with impeccably polished silverware under the glow of a chandelier, spoke of meticulous attention to detail. Everything about the evening felt curated, intentional. He never lacked in the presentation, upmost perfection when it came to the nature of hospitality. He explained that he spent his childhood at his family's resort—a revelation that only deepened my admiration for him. Coincidentally, my own background was rooted in hospitality as well; my very first job, at the age of 13, was bussing tables at a five-star restaurant. This shared experience naturally sparked even more engaging conversation. Edward was unlike anyone I had ever met. His charisma, attentiveness, and genuine warmth made me feel like royalty from the very first moment.

We decided to switch it up from wine to Old Fashions and of course, Edward had perfectly crafted our cocktails; never forgetting to include the large square ice cube and boozy cherries.

As we sat next to each other, both sipping on our cocktails he looked at me in the eyes and simply said, "WOW!" I blushed and asked, "WOW, what?" With a thoughtful nod, he replied, "You're different—in a very good way—but I can't quite explain it yet." I smiled broadly and responded, "Thank you, I think you're quite amazing too, and I'm happy you found me." The evening flowed effortlessly; each moment more entrancing than the last. I thought to myself, "This is too good to be true.".

Between sips of our cocktails, Edward casually mentioned that he'd like to hire an assistant in Las Vegas, especially while he's away traveling. He had recently purchased his home and was busy planning the construction of an additional outdoor patio. He needed someone to be present during the renovations—someone to oversee deliveries of patio furniture and outdoor heaters which would need to be assembled, and other miscellaneous items in preparation for an upcoming company/client party.

He said eagerly, "Come on, I'll show you what I'm envisioning", as we walked outside. He then asks, "Is this something you'd be interested in doing?", "Would $150,000 per year be enough?".

He explained further, "This would be an actual job for you and you wouldn't have to do what you're doing now for money", "And later I'll put you on my company's payroll if you wanted.".

He then leaned in, his eyes looking directly at mine and said, "But I'd need you to be exclusive with me. No other clients." I was taken with surprise and not really taking him seriously. Feeling amused, I said, "You definitely don't waste any time and you don't even know me yet", "It sounds great and I will certainly think about it.", I exclaimed.

He said, "Yes, think about it some more later, then we'll chat again." The thought of one client and the salary seemed ideal to say the least, but I also enjoyed the freedoms I had made for myself. I had become used to not answering to anyone.

I had mixed emotions after Edward's proposal, that of excitement with a bit of apprehensiveness. Unlike the others, Edward didn't just want my company for a night. He wanted me for himself, exclusively. He made an offer I couldn't ignore—a staggering sum that meant I would no longer need to take on other clients. At first, it seemed like security, a step into something more stable. But stability came at a cost.

Considering where my life stood at that time, I was indeed in a vulnerable position and my kindness often has been mistaken by others as weakness, causing some to take it for granted. Over time, I had learned to become fiercely independent and held protective walls after a few fleeting relationships. After nearly a decade of being single—and even a period of 2.5 years immersed in the corporate grind without dating—it sometimes seemed easier to remain solitary. Perhaps, that's why I had chosen to become an escort—to make up for lost time, haha j/k.

It was just before dawn, and as I was leaving Edward's home, he handed me an envelope and asked, "Will that be enough?", I opened the envelope and glanced, noticing several $100 dollar bills, and said, "Absolutely, it's more than enough".

Edward's generosity was undeniable. Yet, as I drove away, I couldn't shake the feeling that this evening marked the beginning of something far more complicated than I initially realized.

4

Stepping Into a Fairy Tale

After meeting with Edward a few more times, I decided to accept his proposal and began working for him. He was a man who always had a plan, never a dull moment—concerts, conferences, sporting events, family and friends visiting, business events, etc. When Edward returned to Las Vegas, fun was his mantra. I remember him telling me he was making up for lost time, having spent much of his childhood working at his father's resort.

He always had something planned, especially for dinner. We frequented the finest five-star restaurants, always accompanied by a bottle of wine. With him, everything was bigger, shinier, more extravagant. He was incredibly flattering, a true charmer, always quick with compliments. He was deeply affectionate, yet never clingy. It wasn't long before I realized I was developing an attraction to Edward. He was starting to grow on me, but as an escort, falling for a client was strictly against the rules for me. Keeping it professional meant drama free.

No sooner had Edward begun saying things like, "Do you know how much?" With a large smile on my face, I asked, "How much, what?" his response was always — "Oh, you'll see." I knew what he meant. But I left it at that. I wasn't ready to go there yet, besides I was still hanging out at Hello.

One morning, as we lay in bed chatting, he mentioned he wanted to expand his real estate investments. Casually, he asked if I could start looking for properties in Las Vegas since I was familiar with the city and had lived there for years. Then, almost offhandedly, he added, "And whatever house you find, I thought you and your daughter could live in it and rent from me."

I hesitated. "That's a possibility, but I'll have to see when my lease is up," I said, brushing it off. It sounded like something he was considering for the distant future, not something urgent. Besides, the idea of living under my client's—or rather, my boss's—roof seemed like too much, too fast.

Two days later, my phone rang. It was Edward, calling from his office in Hilton Head, South Carolina his voice was full of excitement.

Have you started looking for houses yet?!"

His urgency threw me off. "Uhhh… not yet. So, like, ASAP?" I asked, confused.

Trying to get some clarity, I followed up, "Do you have a certain style or preference in mind? And what's the budget?"

Without hesitation, he said, "$700,000."

I blinked. "$700,000?" I repeated, still trying to process what he had just said.

"Okay… so I'm guessing this won't be the house I'll be renting, because I can't afford the rent, much less the utilities."

He said, "We'll figure something out, possibly you could just take care of some of the other expenses…", then with a slight laugh he adds, or we'll work it out in trade."

I was speechless. Part of me was elated—this was a once-in-a-lifetime opportunity. But another part of me couldn't help but wonder: What's the catch?

Edward was still married. I had always preferred not to know whether a client was married or not, it was none of my business. But this situation was different, it entailed far more than just one night. I recall him telling me they had been sleeping in separate rooms for the past five years and that he planned on filing for divorce soon, "But for now," he said, "It's cheaper to keep her".

At the time, I was living in a quaint two-bedroom, one-bath home with real wood flooring. Both the front and backyard were surrounded by beautiful, mature trees, making it feel like anything but the desert. The house was old and built in the late 1950's, but I loved it along with the neighborhood. It reminded me of the older beach homes in California. My front door was painted fuchsia pink, and the house was painted an olive green. I lived a simple life doing art and projects during my off time. I'm very much a free spirit, enjoying anything vintage and unique. I don't go along with the crowd, nor do I require high-end brand names for my things. Well, excluding shoes…lol.

My daughter had been living with me most of the time and we were content, but moving into a larger home was exciting indeed, a dream come true, and even better was seeing her live through this new experience with me.

5

A Hidden Gem

After I got off the phone with Edward, I walked into my daughter's room and said, "So, you know the guy I work for now, Edward? He just gave me a $700,000 budget for a house."

"What?! Are you serious, Mom?!!!" she screamed excitedly.

I had a huge smile and was excited myself, but remained cautious. "Well, nothing is for sure until the day we move in. I'm trying not to get too excited, but let's start looking and see what happens."

Without wasting a second, we both grabbed our laptops and started searching in the zip codes and neighborhoods we knew would be ideal.

I browsed a few listings, but then it clicked—I remembered attending a wedding at my coworker's parents' home. Their property was stunning, located in the same neighborhood as Wayne Newton's estate. I had always loved that area.

And then, less than an hour into our search, there it was.

It was turnkey, exactly what I had envisioned. And the price? Almost perfect.

Before we even reached the freeway, my daughter was already calling the realtor herself. And impressively, she even remembered to mention that it would be a cash deal!

As we approached the property, she gasped with excitement. "Oh my God, Mom! This is the one!"

I nodded, my heart racing. "Wow. I already love it."

We briefly admired it from the outside, eager for our scheduled showing that evening. It was a gorgeous ranch-style home with a guest house, all sitting on a half-acre lot. The pool was breathtaking—something straight out of a resort. The landscaping was pristine, lined with towering palm and pine trees, all mature and lush. It felt like an oasis, almost forgetting I was in the Nevada desert.

I dialed Edward. "We found a house! But… it's a little over budget."

I was nervous. I didn't know him well yet, and it's not every day someone hands you $700,000 and tells you to find a house for them. Still, I was surprised—and impressed—by how much he trusted my judgment in such a short time.

"Great!" he said. "Send me the link! And let me know what you think after you meet with the realtor."

The following morning, Edward wired a deposit. Timing couldn't have been better; the home had fallen out of contract only 4 hours prior to my daughter and I looking at it.

After a few rounds of negotiations with the owner, he paid the rest in full—less than two weeks later. I was stunned. As we chatted on the phone, I couldn't hold back my amazement. "Oh my God, who does that?!".

He laughed and loudly said, "Go big or go home!"

Edward had yet to see the home in person, he was fine with the pictures and videos. He was returning to Vegas in a couple weeks and would see it right before the closing date. Edward was unlike anyone I had ever met; very generous and so quick on the money moves.

6

Unpacking the Future

As I opened my pink front door and stepped inside, I paused, standing still in my living room, inhaling deeply before letting out a slow sigh. "Whew." The house, once a sanctuary, now felt like a temporary stop on a journey I hadn't fully come to terms with. Everything had happened so fast—too fast—and I hadn't given myself the time to process it all. Soon, I'd need to start packing. But for that moment, I stood there, letting the quiet settle around me, waiting for my thoughts to catch up.

I wandered from room to room, trailing my fingers along the edges of my vintage Victorian furnishings, as if committing them to memory. How would I decorate the new place? Would it ever feel like home the way this one did? A bittersweet heaviness settled in my chest. Packing wasn't just about putting things into boxes; it was about deciding what parts of my life to take with me and what to leave behind. Each item I picked up carried weight—not just in my hands but in my heart. Some things felt impossible to part with, while others suddenly seemed like relics from a life that was no longer mine.

My emotions were all over the map—excitement, apprehension, stress, hope—each one crashing into the next. One moment, I'd feel ready, eager to embrace what was ahead; the next, I'd feel fear, as if stepping off a ledge into the unknown. Our relationship hadn't followed a traditional path, and I had to trust that everything would fall into place. But trust was a tricky thing.

It felt like my life had spun on its axis overnight. I was the busiest I'd been in years, waking up early, moving between three houses, my world split across different spaces. And I wasn't even a morning person. My days started at Edward's home on the west side, where the sight of ten or more packages piled up on his porch had become routine.

Upon arrival, I'd greet him through the Ring camera, grinning as I pulled up my blouse to flash him—half hoping, half knowing he was in a meeting or focused on work. He'd get a kick out of it, his voice teasing through the speaker, "Oh great, now I can't go to my meeting until, well… you know." We lived in this flirtatious rhythm, exchanging playful texts, stolen moments of laughter, little ways to brighten each other's day. I loved that I could make him smile, even from miles away, even when he was stuck behind a desk.

But there was an unspoken pressure beneath it all. He wanted everything ready before his guests arrived in town in a couple of weeks. I wanted it all done before he returned. So, I threw myself into the work—assembling outdoor heaters, a dining table, lounge chairs, love seats, a daybed. The physical labor was exhausting but oddly satisfying. Sometimes my daughter and her friend would stop by, their laughter echoing through the backyard as they swam, played music, and soaked in the life Edward had built. Seeing her there made my heart melt. She was busy, doing what teenagers do, preparing to graduate, and I cherished any time I could steal with her.

Edward had a way of getting things done, he had talked the realtor into giving me a key to the new house before the closing date. The moment I stepped inside, it didn't feel real. It most definitely was everything I wanted in a home. But it wasn't mine and I was stepping into his world, not mine. Boxes upon boxes waited for me, stacks of packages growing by the day. It reminded me of opening wedding gifts—exciting, overwhelming, surreal.

UNPACKING THE FUTURE

I remember my daughter walking in, raising her eyebrows. "Mom, more packages?! This is crazy."

I laughed, shaking my head. "I know, I know. I'll need your help opening them. He has more coming tomorrow."

Edward had told me he was ordering kitchen utensils, pots, and pans. "You don't have to do all that," I had told him. "I have plenty of my own."

He responded eagerly, "There will be times when I'm in town, I'll be staying at your house—if you let me, haha. And I'd like to cook for you while I'm there."

He had been a chef at a resort growing up, and I knew how particular he was about food and the tools he used. It was very thoughtful. I even felt relieved—part of me would have been embarrassed for him to use my old, mismatched kitchenware. And besides, it was always nice to have new things in a new home, right?

But as I stood there, surrounded by boxes, something inside me whispered that I was no longer in control, but I did appreciate every bit of it as well. Again, having those bittersweet moments.

The excitement—the thrill of new beginnings—warred with something else. Something quieter, something not revealing itself. It was exhilarating, like stepping into a dream—but also suffocating. My life, my choices, my freedom—little by little, they were being replaced. His world. His rules. His expectations. And maybe I wasn't sure where I fit in anymore.

7

The Tenant with Benefits

It was a perfect spring evening in April, the sky was filled with soft hues of pink and gold as the sun dipped below the mountains. The air was warm, the scent of blooming flowers. Everything about the moment felt picturesque—like a scene out of a movie.

"Cheers!" Edward said, lifting his glass of wine toward mine.

"Cheers," I said, clinking our glasses. "I'm so happy you're back."

We leaned in and kissed. His touch was familiar now, yet something inside me still felt uncertain, as if I were walking a tightrope between fantasy and reality.

"I really missed you," he said.

"I missed you too." The words came easily, but even as I said them, a weight settled deep in my stomach—an unease that had been building beneath the surface.

A long pause stretched between us as I stared down at my glass, swirling the deep red liquid inside. My heart pounded. I took a deep breath, steadying myself.

"There's something I need to talk to you about."

Edward appearing puzzled. I saw the flicker of something in his eyes—was it curiosity? Or was it warning?

I continued, my voice sounding nervous. "Everything has happened so fast for me—for us. I haven't had the time to fully process it. I haven't even spent enough time with you to truly trust you."

My throat tightened, but I forced myself to continue. "I need some sort of guarantee that once I move into your house, my daughter and I won't be left out in the cold."

Edward remained silent, watching me.

I exhaled shakily, my voice breaking. "You're married, Edward. And you told me your wife doesn't know about your properties here in Las Vegas—but how do I know she won't show up one day? How do I know I won't be blindsided, forced to start over yet again?"

Tears already in my eyes before I could stop them. I hated showing this kind of vulnerability, but it was all too much, so fast.

Edward let out a slow breath, setting his wine glass down. "I'm not obligated to tell her anything. It's none of her business. Our finances are separate, and I will divorce her when the time is right. Heck, I'd divorce her today if I could." His voice was calm, measured reassuring, but also distant.

I wanted to believe him. I needed to believe him. But something about his certainty unnerved me.

"I understand that," I said, "but there are too many variables at play. I've worked too hard to rebuild my life, and I won't risk my daughter's stability. I need something solid—a contract, something in writing."

He leaned back, considering. "How about I provide you with a lease for now? We can work on the rest later."

I nodded slowly, though the unease didn't fade. "That'll be fine. I'm sorry… it's just a lot for me right now, I'm not used to someone doing all this for me."

He grabbed my hand and held it, his touch warm, reassuring. "Don't worry about a thing, It always works out. All I want to do is make you happy."

He smiled and said, "Okay? Everything will be okay."

But looking back, that conversation was the first of many moments where I should have seen the cracks forming beneath the surface. He had presented it as a simple arrangement—I would be both a tenant and an employee. The tenant with benefits. It all appeared so innocent. But the reality was much different.

In truth, I was about to move in with a man I barely knew on a deep level. A man who had yet to truly reveal himself to me. It was all so foreign, yet I kept telling myself it would be okay. I wanted it to be okay.

I longed for real, uninterrupted time together—time to grow closer, to build something real. But there was always that one glaring truth I couldn't ignore: he was still married and was there more to the story?

So, what exactly was I to him? A girlfriend? A placeholder? A carefully curated escape from the life he claimed he didn't want? Or was I something else entirely—his personal indulgence, his possession, an extension of his carefully controlled world?

Finding balance felt impossible. The moment I thought I understood my place, the ground shifted beneath me again. And yet, Edward knew exactly how to keep me in place. He knew the right things to say, the right gestures to make.

"You must know how special you are to me," he would whisper. "I adore you. My goal this year, among others, is to make you happy."

"When I see you happy and smiling, it makes me happy."

"There isn't anything I won't do for you."

His voice, his words, his presence—they were like a spell, wrapping around me, pulling me in deeper.

He carried a sense of innocence; a polished sincerity that made it all feel real. My family adored him, saw only the version of him that he wanted them to see; all while I saw different, but couldn't question on something I had yet to understand.

But there I was, sitting across from him on that warm spring evening, wine in hand, the scent of flowers lingering in the air, feeling the weight of something I couldn't yet name. Vulnerability. Instability. The quiet realization that I had just handed my life over to someone who had never truly let me in, but everything on the outside, my surroundings, this material world was perfect.

8

Under the Radar, Over the Moon

Edward had been in town alone for a few days without friends or family, and finally, I had the chance to spend some quality time with him. Don't get me wrong—I loved his friends and family—but I wanted to know Edward, the real Edward.

As we prepared for his business gathering, we went grocery shopping and ran errands together. Those simple moments are what I cherished. With Edward, a routine trip to the grocery store was like going to an amusement park. Sometimes we'd first stop at the bar and start with a cocktail, play Keno, then go shopping. We'd laugh, flirt, and joke with each other like kids. When things were good between us, they were completely, unequivocally good—unlike anything I had ever experienced.

We found a bartender for the party, and I was going to help as well, but Edward preferred I come as a guest too. He was excited to introduce me to everyone even though we had to keep things under the radar. I always made sure I was prepared for the audience I'd be introduced to, and I would ask Edward, "What will you be telling everyone who I am?" and "Where did we meet?" I wanted our stories to align. After all, these were his clients, colleagues, and employees.

I admired Edward's ability to host a gathering so well; he did it with grace. He liked things to be perfect—just as I did. We made a great team when it came to entertaining. Our rhythm was seamless: he prepared hors d'oeuvres and the main course while I cleaned and decorated.

When Edward entered a room, everyone knew it; he had this presence about him that exuded confidence. It was his charisma and charm—he made everyone feel like his best friend. I loved that about him, it's what made me truly attracted to him. Especially, when we would both gaze at each other from across the room with flirtatious gestures.

After the guests had left, it was just the two of us alone in the kitchen listening to music. A little tipsy, we swayed together, slow dancing. Then, he stopped, looked into my eyes, and held me close.

"I love you", he said. "I know it sounds crazy and too soon, but I'm falling in love with you".

I began to cry; they were tears of happiness. I said, "Oh my God, I'm falling in love with you too. I love you".

He kissed me, and we stood there wrapped in each other's arms. Then he asked, "Can we stop with the professional relationship thing? I want us to be committed to each other, to be in a real relationship. I know it doesn't sound right since I'm still married, but I'm working on that."

I was so happy, I needed to know where I stood with him, especially as my feelings deepened. The doubts and fears I had before had somehow subsided. I felt a sense of peace and security.

"I would love that for us.", I told him.

At that moment, I felt euphoric, I felt complete. But unfortunately, that feeling wasn't there to stay.

9

Unspoken Promises

I've recently deepened my understanding of the dynamic between super empaths and those with narcissistic tendencies. It can be a turbulent relationship, but once both surpass the initial hurdles, it can be a very powerful one as well. Essentially, both personalities are 180 degrees apart, whereas they could almost compensate for each other's strengths and weaknesses entirely. It is an incredibly delicate balance where empathy and manipulation intersect. A super empath is easily willing to put others' needs before their own, whereas someone with narcissistic tendencies is driven by self-interest. If I had done the inner work years ago and recognized my own patterns, I might have been able to manage my reactions more effectively, especially when dealing with someone like Edward.

Edward was back in Hilton Head, South Carolina, and this was the first time we had been apart since becoming more serious in our relationship. I had two weeks to be completely moved out of my house into the new one. I had never been so busy in my life. I kept telling myself and my daughter that I couldn't wait for us to be settled in and finally able to relax.

In the midst, of moving, I recall the "west wing," lol, of the house having a major plumbing issue. I sent Edward pictures of the mess, saying, "Hi, it's me, Cinderella, we have an issue." Not only was I in the middle of moving, but

I also needed a plumber. Then, the doorbell rang—it was the home sound system guys, arriving to do the install throughout the house and backyard. Chaos surrounded me, and my parents stopped by to help as well. Soon after, one of the guys walked through the front door and asked, "Where would you like these Amazon packages?" Oh, and to top it off, the patio furniture was arriving at the same time. Then, my phone rang. It was Edward. He had been out on a fishing boat with the guys all day and proceeded to tell me, "I'll be coming back a week early. I have some friends visiting, but they'll be staying at my house." Looking back, that day was comical in its own hectic way.

Edward had a childlike attitude. He was always thinking ahead and making plans, acting as everyone's personal travel agent. He took control of all our flights, set up mine and my family's SkyMiles accounts, arranged TSA, and made sure to plan our annual vacations perfectly. I appreciated and admired that part of him, among many other things. He made our life exciting, but at times, it was too busy for me. I longed for quiet nights, just the two of us, relaxing around the house and watching a movie. Our relationship had yet to find the horse for the cart—yes, I know, we put the cart before the horse.

After a few days of him being away in South Carolina, I began to notice a shift. Edward became distant on the phone, and the number of daily messages decreased significantly. The tone went from flirty and romantic to one-word responses. Sometimes, I wouldn't hear from him for a day, at times almost two. Then, I'd wake up to at least ten messages and a couple of voicemails, all over-the-top flirty and romantic again. And this cycle would repeat every few days. I wasn't needy and didn't require constant attention, but his inconsistencies and patterns, coupled with my intuition, were sending me signals.

One day, I called Edward. He sent a message: "Call you in 10 min, in a meeting." Five hours passed. Frustrated, I decided to voice my thoughts and sent him this: "I believe our relationship should return to a professional one. When I commit to someone, I open my heart and soul to them. It's difficult for me to truly trust this situation, and at times, I feel I'm being played."

His response, a couple hours later, "I've been crying for the past hour. I'm devastated. Being played is a complete mischaracterization of the facts. I've been open and honest with you about everything, including my deep feelings and love for you."

Edward hadn't slept well the night before and said his stomach was in knots and that he'd hate it if I needed to take a step backwards with our relationship. He professed his love to me with sincerity. I felt bad and apologized for jumping to conclusions realizing it must be due to my past trust issues. But I didn't forget about that gut feeling; when you know, you know.

Fast forward three years, Edward had given me his passcode to his phone and insisted I could go through it whenever I wanted. What I found didn't surprise me.

As I perused through the history, there were emails exchanged between him and one of his regular escorts arranging appointments throughout that same week. I cross-referenced the dates and times with the messages between him and I. As he was telling me how much he loved me, r sent her the same pic that he sent me, within a couple minutes apart, he was messaging her. Then, during the time frame he was ghosting me, not only matched with the dates and time frame he arranged to be with her, also matched with my messages to him regarding my doubts with our relationship, and I'm being played, etc.

This wasn't the only instance I found. There were several others, but at the time I had nothing to rely on except my gut feeling. Still, the emotional toll of trying to hold everything inside was immense. My frustrations would eventually boil over, leading me to question him abruptly, making accusations towards him. Heated arguments would erupt, often ending with me flying back to Las Vegas.

After every argument, Edward would shut off my credit card and stop my checks, leaving me emotionally and financially stranded. All while I'm flooding his phone with my frustrations and angry text messages, he'd ignore me for days or even weeks, giving me the silent treatment.

Eventually, guilt would overwhelm me, especially after being told I was "delusional" or that I had "blown things out of proportion." I'd apologize, promising to manage my emotions better. Almost instantly, Edward would respond, showering me with love, flowers, or money—as though nothing had happened. He never wanted to discuss the arguments. "It's the past, let's just be happy," he'd say.

He would tell me that the reasoning for the silence was because my words were offensive to him, or he wanted to wait until I cooled down. Only later did I realize that during those silent stretches, he was with other women.

This was the pattern, I held us together emotionally, loving him unconditionally and in return I received the material world. It took me a long time to fully grasp the depth of it, and tolerating it was a challenge for me. I kept trying though.

10

Illusion of Abundance

Edward and my daughter shared a unique bond, which comforted me deeply. I remember one afternoon, as we chatted in the dining room while he juggled work calls, he asked me to go over our upcoming travel dates. When I mentioned that my daughter's 18th birthday would fall during one of our trips, his eyes lit up. "Do you have something planned?!" he asked.

"I was thinking of booking one of those exotic suites on the Strip for her and her friends, or maybe doing a surprise party at the house," I replied.

"Yes! And I'll have a band come play too!" he said excitedly.

"You don't have to do that. They can hook up their music here—that's what the sound system is for," I said.

He paused for a moment. "Wait, doesn't she like the Red Hot Chili Peppers? Let me see if I can get them to come."

"What?! No, that's crazy!" I laughed as he started typing on his computer, pulling up their website. Eventually, we realized it would cost far too much, along with many other demands.

I was grateful for his willingness to make her birthday special, but I also didn't want him to feel like he needed to impress her with such extravagant gestures. He often brushed off my concerns, saying things like, "This is what I do," or "Can't I do what I want to do? It's what makes me happy." So, I let him run with it.

Later, my daughter came to me and said, "I don't really need a big party. I don't have that many friends, and if Edward is willing to spend that kind of money, I'd rather have a new car."

I left it up to them, and they eventually found a $65,000 car. She was ecstatic and deeply grateful, and I was genuinely happy for her.

Yet, beneath the surface, I began to feel like I was losing control—not just of my life, but of my daughter's as well. I felt insignificant. I started questioning whether it was all genuine or part of something deeper. I wasn't prepared for her to be exposed to such materialism. I feared it might distort her beliefs, convincing her that life should always come with such excess. The reality was, I was trying to protect her from an illusion that was only beginning to reveal itself to me.

Edward's generosity extended beyond birthdays. Holidays were his favorite time of year, especially as a chef, he had a knack for perfection. Thanksgiving and Christmas dinners were culinary masterpieces. The gifts piled so high we struggled to fit them under the tree. It was far from normal, but undeniably exciting. Most of all, those moments gave me precious time with both my son and my daughter, something I now deeply cherish. As adults living in different parts of the world, they are pursuing their dreams and building their own lives. I am beyond proud of them and love them deeply.

I remember our first Christmas together vividly. After we finished opening gifts, Edward handed me an envelope. Inside was a clever riddle he had written, hinting at what to do next. It turned out to be the start of a scavenger hunt, each envelope leading to another. I was impressed with Edward's creativity and selflessly taking the time for it all. When I finally reached the last one, I found a key to a 2022 Corvette Stingray inside. I was shocked and so excited, but soon after followed mixed emotions. Beneath the excitement, there was an unexpected sense of guilt. I felt indebted, as though I needed to be more and do more for Edward. While this being such an extravagant gesture, I was beyond grateful and admired Edward for everything he had already done for myself and my family. If it had been a matter of still trying to impress me, I was already impressed long before.

Edward provided me with a lavish lifestyle, make no mistake, but our perception of love didn't align. For me, no amount of luxury could replace the missing piece I so desired; I needed true love in return, Edward's heart. I battled with him telling me he loved me, then the quiet knowing that other women were a part of his life also. For me, that was like trying to mix oil and water— the chemistry won't allow it. Even during the happiest moments, it made it impossible for me to feel pure joy. I found myself wondering when my time was up for replacement causing me to hesitate, never allowing myself to become too complacent with a life of uncertainty. I was catapulted into a competition, an unspoken competition that I never agreed to. But still, I felt I had to accept it and the pain that would go along with it.

Edward's need for constant admiration and validation—a hallmark of those with narcissistic tendencies—was apparent. Over time, I began withholding that admiration, not out of malice, but as an unconscious reaction to his lack of honesty. My emotional withdrawal likely left him feeling unappreciated, prompting him to seek validation elsewhere.

We were caught in an endless cycle, stuck in the law of motion: for every action, there is an equal or opposite reaction.

11

Curiosity Killed the Trust

I always knew Edward had escorts in his contact list—hundreds of them. Their names were coded, cleverly disguised with city abbreviations added to a first name, like "Mia-NY" or "LVAshley." It wasn't a surprise. He was a very wealthy man. With his resources, he could afford anyone. I was understanding of his past; it was the present that concerned me. I told myself it was history—irrelevant to what we were trying to build today.

But three months before the holidays, something shifted.

A gut feeling nudged me to check his search history. I wasn't looking to create a problem—I just couldn't shake the sense that something was off. And there it was: escort websites.

I confronted him.

He looked at me with that cold calmness and said, "I was just curious."

"Curious?" I repeated, trying to steady my voice. "Curious if the grass is greener, is how I see it."

"No, not at all," he said dismissively. "I was just wondering what they're up to. They're my friends."

"Possibly, you could text them and ask directly because escorts don't necessarily let people know their personal life on their websites.", I told him.

"Remember, how we met?", I asked him.

He denied it all. Insisted there was nothing behind it. No plans. No intentions. Again, I swept it under the rug. I waited until the holidays passed and had the urge to go through Edward's phone. I didn't want to disrupt the holidays because I knew there would be things I'd find and it would have ruined my family's holiday as well.

He had reached out to one of them. His "curiosity" turned out to be a real arrangement or rather attempting to. When I confronted him again, he was quick with another excuse: it was for his brother. "He didn't have a membership," Edward said, as if that made it logical.

That was always Edward's game—excuses dressed up as explanations.

He thought I was like all the others. He expected me to stay quiet, to submit, to play the role. But I wasn't naive. I wasn't blind. And I refused to pretend his lies were truth.

Still, he didn't stop at denial. He shifted blame onto me, weaponizing my emotions against me:

"You're sick. You need help."

"You're so insecure. So jealous."

"When will you ever be happy?"

"You're probably the one cheating—people who accuse are usually guilty themselves."

When that didn't work, he threw money in my face:

"I bought you a house."

"I gave you a Corvette."

"I got your daughter a car."

"I put carpet in your parents' house."

"I pay for everyone's flights and vacations."

He made it sound like love was transactional. That because he gave, I should be silent. Grateful. Obedient.

But none of it was truly mine. The house, the car—nothing was in my name. It was all conditional. I could use them, so long as I stayed. So long as I tolerated. So long as I played my part in his carefully constructed illusion.

To the outside world, it looked like I was living a dream. But inside, I was suffocating in silence. I was paying the emotional price.

There isn't a single person who will ever truly understand the depth of pain I endured—unless they've experienced betrayal from someone they deeply, desperately loved. I tried to get him to listen, to see me, to understand what he was doing to my heart. But in his eyes, I had become the enemy. The one who kept him from doing whatever he pleased. Although, it was okay that he trampled on my heart over and over with no regard how I felt about it. I wanted him to understand and know who I truly was from the inside.

I didn't want a perfect man—I wanted an honest one. A man who valued respect. A partner who wouldn't gamble with my health and well-being for his momentary pleasure. Once again, I felt empty and alone; then, finding myself isolated.

I remained in Las Vegas while he traveled back to South Carolina. I remember reaching out to my family for their opinion and they'd tell me things like:

"You've always had trust issues."

"Why would he do so much for us if he wanted someone else?"

"Edward's such a nice person—he's not like that."

"You know men… they all cheat."

As if betrayal was normal. As if lying was part of the deal. As if money made it all okay, while I take one for the team! Edward walked through life with a godlike complex—entitled, untouchable, unaccountable—expecting everyone to submit to his rules while he broke every one of mine. It's not what I signed up for.

I'm not someone who lives for appearances. I live in the truth. I don't need lavish gifts—I need respect. The person that claims to love me doesn't put my health and emotional safety at risk for their own selfish instant gratifying pleasures. To anyone who envied me—who thought I had it all—I'd say: you can have it. I invite you to take my place.

The most devastating part wasn't even his betrayal—it was how he seeped into the very core, the foundation of my life and fractured what I held most sacred: my family. He took control of not only my life, but my family. Edward didn't have a strong foundation set forth from childhood that consisted of a close family unit, one of which nurtured, instilled morals, values, a healthy belief system, and most importantly, love. And by bringing him into our world, I exposed my family to something toxic. Something that would eventually erode my relationships—not just with friends, but with my children.

And that is a wound I still carry.

12

The Noise in His Silence

Edward apologized and promised he wouldn't betray me in any way, shape, or form. I accepted. I truly believed our relationship would work—partly because I thought I was finally starting to understand why he did the things he did, even if they weren't right.

I didn't realize it as it was happening, but now I see how he love bombed me—and how easily I got pulled back in. He had a way of making me feel the same way I did when we first met, recreating that early spark. I didn't realize I was being drawn back into the same never-ending cycle. My intuition tried to warn me, but I ignored it. That newness felt too good. It gave me a high—like a bad drug—and this time, it seemed we were stronger. I recall him telling me, "This isn't a formal proposal, however I want you to know that I want us to get married in the near future. Once I retire, that's where I want us to be."

Not only would the love bombing suck me back in, I remember the first night we met, and Edward told me, "I've always needed more than just one woman in my life", "I'm not sure why, but I believe it's due to abandonment issues during my childhood.", he said. That always stuck in my head, often finding myself reflecting on that moment, believing I could remedy his past wounds. It was one of the few times he spoke with pure authenticity; one of the rare moments he was vulnerable. But I now see why, I wasn't a threat to him, I was a stranger that wasn't going to judge him. He felt safe with me then.

We moved forward with our trip to Argentina. We were gone for 11 days, and it was the best vacation we'd ever taken together. Edward planned everything. We flew private, and the jet was incredible—intimate, luxurious, perfect.

Flying over the Caribbean was unlike anything I'd ever seen. I've always admired the ocean, especially the way the different shades of blue shift beneath the sun. The water was so clear, it looked like mountain ranges beneath the surface.

After landing at the main airport, we hopped in a helicopter that took us to the resort. I remember how windy it was as we crossed the bay—gusts of wind tossed us around like a kite in the air. Edward and I exchanged nervous glances. The pilot and the helicopter were both up there in age, and later Edward joked, "I kept thinking, what if this guy has a heart attack and I have to fly it?" I had thought the same and was already putting an exit plan together in my head. It was a scary ride for sure.

The scenery was lush and wild—thick, jungle-like foliage stretched for miles. As we approached the landing pad, it looked like we were headed straight into the trees. We gave each other a look like, WTF? Then, suddenly, a small clearing appeared—just big enough for the helicopter. The pilot landed it perfectly. He knew exactly what he was doing.

Spending more than a few days alone with Edward always seemed to strengthen our bond. It was the only time I had his full presence, and I could feel the difference. His emotions matched his outer self, that's when I knew he was being genuine. It was a temporary breath of fresh air that I savored as long as I could.

Like I've said before—when our relationship was good, it was really good. Edward would say things like, "I love when we get along. I love when we're happy," and I'd agree. I cherished those moments.

But now I know—I wasn't able to make Edward as happy as he needed to be and the same goes with myself; he wasn't able to make me as happy as I needed to be. He needed to practice self-love, and I needed to learn how to save love for myself and not feel guilty and emotionally depleted.

I wasn't perfect—but I didn't run. I've made mistakes, I've felt heartbreak. But I've also sat in silence with my pain. I've cried and prayed and held myself when no one else did. I've asked hard questions and let the answers break me open. That's not weakness. That's self-love.

Edward wasn't used to someone like me. I refused to wear the rose-tinted glasses and take advantage of him for his money like the rest of the women did. I was the opposite. While Edward desired someone that "needed" him, yes, they needed his money, but he saw it differently. That's because the others were telling him what he wanted to hear, gave him the admiration that he so desired. All but to blind him of what was really going on. I didn't need Edward, I wanted him.

Edward didn't know how to be alone for very long, he wasn't comfortable in his own skin, and I know he didn't prefer silence. Walking on the beach was the most Edward allowed himself to be in solitude, in his own thoughts and afterwards he'd tell me how energetic and relaxed he felt. But no sooner, he needed to distract himself from the emotions seeping in that he had been pushing aside for so long. It was avoidance. A fear of sitting still long enough to feel. I knew there was a lot for him to release and we as humans are creatures of habit. We can become comfortable, being miserable avoiding change out of fear.

He wore his charm like armor. But real strength isn't loud—it's honest. It's quiet. It's the decision to stay present, even when the emotions are messy.

Self-love was something that I didn't have a clear understanding until recently. Self-love is healing past emotional wounds by acknowledging, facing, and releasing them. As a safety mechanism, a person might embed the emotional pain so deep that they have no memory of such other than their childhood was unpleasant. These unhealed traumas or dark attachments are likely to cause a deep energetic void inside. As they develop into adulthood, that wound is often covered with charm, control, and grandiosity —but underneath is a deep sense of shame, fear, or emotional abandonment.

Until a person is healed from trauma, they cannot generate light energy due to the blockages within their soul energy field, chakras. Depending on the level of trauma, these dark voids or attachments can't generate its own light—it can only feed off it. Some might call them energy vampires. If someone is carrying heavy, dark energy, and they encounter someone radiant and grounded in light, they experience temporary relief, healing, or even euphoria just by being near them. That light feels like salvation, but if they're not ready to rise to that vibration themselves, they start to rely on the other person as the source—rather than doing the work to generate their own.

As a super empath, my energy is like a beacon. Edward's narcissistic tendencies sensed this, consciously or not. I provided what he could not access himself—validation, love, warmth, unconditional acceptance. This created a cycle where I'd give and he'd take, leaving me drained and him temporarily "fed." Edward lacked emotional receptivity, so he didn't understand my love; he couldn't feel my love emotionally, he absorbed it energetically. And sadly, he returned his love monetarily because that's all he knew.

It saddens me knowing that someone is willing to live their life never feeling the most important emotions that life offers due to fear of facing repressed trauma. God so graciously gave love, compassion, empathy; all of which are priceless. I just wish he knew what he was missing because my only wish was to help him heal; that's why I kept returning.

THE NOISE IN HIS SILENCE

He wasn't in love with me—he was in love with how he felt around me. And what he felt... was my light quieting his darkness.

13

A Soul's Quiet Escape

We were back in Hilton Head, SC where Edward purchased a condo on the beach once his divorce was final. Edward walked through the front door like he always did after being at the office all day. Same smile, same *happy* tone in his voice, but something felt different, and I couldn't identify it, but I knew it wasn't good. I felt uneasy, agitated—right when he stood in the foyer taking his shoes off. Something about him was... off.

I stood there and I could feel a puzzled look on my face, unsure of why my body had tensed, why my heart was racing when nothing had happened. He greeted me like normal, maybe a little distracted. But that wasn't new. Still, I couldn't shake it. An unfamiliar weight that was hovering, it felt tense.

I poured us both a glass of wine and hoped it would take the edge off. Then, I made a cocktail. That uneasy feeling wouldn't go away. We planned on going for a walk again on the beach, but Edward wanted to rest, and I decided I'd go sit by the pool. Oddly enough, I immediately felt better once I got outside in the sun.

By the time we went to bed, I couldn't sleep. Anxiety was running through my veins. I felt panicky for no reason. The longer I laid there, the worse it got—until my head began to pound. A full-blown migraine crept in. I couldn't remember the last time I had a migraine, and it was the kind that you need complete darkness.

I got out of bed and laid down on the floor. Somehow, the ground felt better. Calmer. Cooler. Then, I thought to myself, maybe it's my blood pressure, so I got up to check it and it was fine. I eventually took half of a Xanex to calm my nerves. The next morning when I woke up, I felt fine. Edward wasn't there, he already left to go to the office. However, once he got home, I felt a little on edge, but it could have been due to me getting things ready since we had friends coming to visit for the weekend.

Two days later, while we were at dinner with our friends, suddenly I began bleeding — profusely. I was wearing a white summer dress. Talk about embarrassing, but there wasn't time for me to worry. Edward took me to the emergency room. The doctor returned with my lab work, and he told me that I had an infection, and that the bleeding was likely premenopausal. But something in me knew better. I've always been in tune with my body and this felt almost foreign.

The antibiotics helped, and after a week or so, I started to feel more like myself again. The bleeding stopped, the weight on my chest lifted—at least temporarily. I remember thinking maybe it had all been in my head. Stress. Hormones. The doctors were probably right. But just when I started to find a sense of calm again, another strange physical symptom appeared.

I woke up one morning with a sharp pain shooting from my neck through my shoulder and down my arm. My entire right side felt tight, heavy, and partially numb. I kept trying to stretch it, shake it out—nothing helped. It came out of nowhere as though I pulled a muscle lifting heavy weights. Ironically, Edward had been complaining about shoulder pain too and he had gone to doctor for an examine.

My symptoms vanished just as suddenly as they had arrived, a few days later. But the timing felt odd—too coincidental to ignore. It was like I was physically mirroring him. Absorbing what he wouldn't say out loud. This was something I would come to understand more fully later: the way energy entangles when one partner is open and empathic, and the other is guarded and dishonest.

As an empath, I had always been sensitive to the emotions and energy of others, but this experience taught me something new—something *vital*. We are not just physical beings. We are energetic bodies, too. And when our light is pure and open, it becomes a magnet not just for love, but also for energetic interference. Especially from those who carry unresolved darkness. Especially from those with narcissistic tendencies and the residue that can become parasitic whose energy is often fractured, toxic, and deeply unstable.

Weeks passed, and one morning, I found myself awake long before the sun. Restless again. My thoughts were erratic, my chest tight. That old anxiety had returned. Edward was still asleep. I slipped out of bed and moved quietly through the kitchen, deciding to make him coffee. Maybe a small act of kindness would soften the energy that had grown increasingly cold between us.

When I brought it to him, I found him in the closet, wrapped in a towel. His back was turned, and he was holding his phone—so fixated on whatever he was doing that he didn't hear me walk in. I watched in silence as he quickly slid the phone into his sock drawer and closed it. Like nothing had happened.

I held out the mug. "Here's your coffee."

He turned slowly; his expression smooth. Too smooth. His voice was sweet and calm, "Hi, baby."

I smiled and kissed him on the cheek, pretending I hadn't seen anything. I didn't have the energy to confront him—not then. Especially not with a business gathering to attend that evening. I had learned the hard way that asking the wrong question at the wrong time could implode an entire night.

But later that morning, something else caught my attention. Edward had left me a voice message—it sounded like he was in a parking garage. I could hear background noise. The sound of car doors. A brief conversation. He told someone thank you, and I clearly heard him tipping a valet attendant.

He had told me he'd be in the office all morning, buried in meetings. No time to talk. He didn't say anything about leaving. But that audio clip told a different story.

That night, after the business event, I couldn't hold it in any longer. Once again, the adrenaline running through my body, no surprise, it was par for the course. I couldn't maintain a fake smile and play nice any longer.

I looked at him and asked, "Why were you hiding your phone in your sock drawer this morning?"

He blinked, and said, "Huh?", "What are you talking about?"

"I saw you. I was standing right there."

"Ohhhhh, here we go again with your crazy premonition crap." he said, as he deflected.

"And where were you this morning?" I asked, my tone calm, even though I could feel the blood rushing through my temples.

"You said you never left the office, but I heard you on the voice message. You were tipping valet. Where were you really?"

He gave a partial shrug. "You're overthinking again. You always do this."

Gaslighting. A familiar deflection. Trying to confuse me, make me question myself, my memory, my own instincts.

But my body had already answered for me. It had been answering for weeks. Every ache, every wave of anxiety, every unexplained migraine and numbness—none of it was random. It was my light, my soul warning me. My spirit had been sounding alarms long before I found evidence with my eyes.

That's the thing about energy. It doesn't lie. Words can. Smiles can. Even actions can be staged. But energy? Energy always tells the truth.

And when you are a person of light—of deep emotional and spiritual sensitivity—you will feel the storm before it hits. You'll feel the betrayal before it has a name. You'll feel the truth before it's ever spoken.

What I learned during those moments—those seemingly small betrayals—is that light and dark cannot peacefully coexist. Dark energy feeds off of light, often without ever acknowledging it. It pulls, drains, consumes—slowly, subtly, until one day, you no longer recognize the radiant, vibrant version of yourself you once were.

That morning, in the closet, I watched Edward's energy shift. I saw how smooth he was with his lie. How calm he could remain while concealing something. And I also saw how, yet again, I had swallowed my truth to avoid making him uncomfortable. But every time we do that—swallow truth, dim our light, doubt what we know—we give our energy away. Piece by piece. Until our body becomes the battlefield for a war we didn't even agree to fight.

We slept in separate rooms that night. There was no shouting, no slamming of doors—just a quiet, heaviness in the air, very distant. I lay in bed, staring at the ceiling, knowing deep inside that something had shifted permanently. My body was tired. I had been here before—packing my things, making an exit—but this time felt different.

A SOUL'S QUIET ESCAPE

This time, I just wanted to escape and have peace.

While Edward slept, I moved through the condo, arms full of clothing, quietly tiptoeing into the guest room to begin packing. I didn't cry. I didn't hesitate. I was numb, but not in a disconnected way—more like laser-focused determination. I was finally listening to the voice inside me that had been warning me for months.

That was the thing about Edward—he seemed to feed off of it. Drama. Confusion. Half-truths. It was always something. And I realized then that people like him don't just create chaos for the thrill—they create it to keep your energy tethered to theirs. As long as I was dizzy from the storm, I couldn't see clearly enough to leave.

But I wasn't dizzy anymore. I was awake. And I was done.

I packed as much as I could. The rest I stuffed into boxes and prepped for shipping. I had made my decision: I was driving the Corvette back to Las Vegas. He gave it to me for Christmas, but I knew if I left it behind, he'd find a way to keep it. I also knew that if I told him I was leaving, he'd try to talk me out of it. Or worse—guilt me, confuse me, reel me back in with promises that would evaporate days later.

So I didn't say a word.

The next morning, after he left for the office, I drove to UPS and dropped off the boxes. I returned to the condo, loaded the Corvette with the rest of my things, didn't think twice, and I pulled away. No goodbye. No closure. Just silence and an open road ahead.

Once I got on the highway, I felt free, it was therapeutic. Having time in my own thoughts was peaceful. I didn't have someone telling me what I should feel and how I should react, that isn't healthy.

I hit a bad rainstorm in Mobile, AL, and couldn't see more than three feet in front of me, so I trailed 15 mph behind a semi, his lights were guiding me. It cleared up shortly thereafter. Around 1 a.m., I stopped in Dallas and spent the night. I got about four hours of sleep, then I was right back on the highway. I stopped just outside of Amarillo, in Childress, TX to stretch. I bought me a few pairs of cowboy boots. Retail therapy is great for the soul. It made me feel good and I can never pass up a good sale.

Once I crossed the state line into New Mexico, the tears came. Coming home always made me feel sentimental, but this time was different. The emotion hit deeper. It reminded me of when I was little—how my dad would hold me close when I was upset, and the moment I felt safe in his arms, I'd cry even harder. As if his embrace gave me permission to finally let it all out. That's what this drive felt like. Like safety. Like release. And it felt so good to finally cry.

I got off on the next exit in Santa Rosa for gas and from there, I got back on the road. I drove all the way through to Las Vegas except to gas up one more time. The mountains, the silence, the night sky—was so peaceful, the whole drive was an experience, I'll always remember.

I made it back to Las Vegas in just two and a half days. Alone. But not lonely. What I've come to understand is that protecting your light is about recognizing when your nervous system is warning you, when your energy feels invaded—your body knows. Your energy knows.

14

No Fairy Tale Ending Here

When I got home and walked through the door, I exhaled. My place in Las Vegas felt like sacred ground—safe, familiar. The energy was lighter. Still, a strange kind of silence filled the space. I placed my things on the bench in the foyer.

I was relieved, yes—but I was also nervous. Even scared. Because the truth is, when you've spent a couple years of being manipulated, gaslit, and emotionally spun in circles, freedom doesn't always feel like freedom at first. It feels like withdrawal. Like floating in unfamiliar space without the chaos you've become addicted to. I was untethered.

By the time I made it home, Edward and I had exchanged a handful of texts. Cold. Dismissive. Defensive. He denied everything I had seen through my own eyes. He told me I was imagining it all, that I was delusional, unstable. Yet again, projecting out to me that *I* needed help and should seek counseling.

The worst part wasn't even his denial. It was the way he flipped the narrative so effortlessly, like he'd rehearsed it. One minute he was playing victim, the next he was the accuser. He said he couldn't live like this anymore. That *I* was the one who brought chaos into *his* life. That *I* needed to work on myself.

And a part of me—fragile, still healing—believed him. That's what emotional abuse does. It breaks down your self-esteem so slowly, so methodically, that by the time you try to leave, you don't recognize yourself anymore. You second-guess everything. Even your truth. Even your sanity.

I had become co-dependent without even realizing it. I had started to believe I couldn't function without his validation, his affection, even his attention—whether it came in the form of love or cruelty. When you're starved for peace long enough, chaos begins to feel like home. And in his world, love always came with pain.

That first night alone in the home that I thought was a dream come true, was in fact a dream and only a dream. Actually, it was becoming a fairy tale with a bad ending. I felt like someone had just dropped me off in the middle of a world I couldn't even name, and there wasn't a soul that existed. I couldn't go to the man that I still loved and explain the hurt and pain I felt, hoping he'd finally listen and understand. I could talk with family and friends, but it was the same old story different day. Besides, we're wasting each others time discussing something that only I had the capacity to figure out. I'm the only one that knows what will be the best for me and that's where solitude and isolation is necessary. It's the only way I can find the answers.

Had I known then what I know now, I would've realized I was trauma bonded. A concept I had never heard of, let alone understood. I couldn't comprehend the amount of destruction that had been occurring repeatedly, effecting my inner world and my outer reality. I had been turned inside out as though my soul had vanished, feeling lost, and abandoned. Possibly, I had become the person that Edward was hiding under the mask. He molded me into his own image—into what he feared for himself the most.

A trauma bond occurs when periods of intense love and excitement are followed by emotional neglect, manipulation, and mistreatment. This cycle of devaluation and reward creates a powerful chemical and hormonal attachment. Our brains become addicted to the chemicals produced during each phase of the trauma bond:

- **Oxytocin** (bonding)
- **Endogenous opioids** (pleasure, pain, withdrawal, dependence)
- **Corticotropin-releasing factor** (stress)
- **Dopamine** (craving, seeking, wanting)

With such a strong neurochemical cocktail, emotions become nearly impossible to regulate—and making logical decisions becomes a struggle. That's why I kept going back. It became my normal. I didn't know any better.

Trauma bonding often starts with intense admiration: love bombing. Compliments. Generosity. Chivalry. A manipulative tactic designed to gain rapid trust and emotional dependence.

Then, slowly, comes the devaluation. The testing. For instance, he might take you to a place he's been before, but you haven't. The bartender is beautiful. He flirts with her. Excludes you from the conversation. And when you try to interject, he looks at you with contempt. You're stunned. After all, you've been his queen—believing he'd never hurt you. But this is where the shift begins.

Once they know they've got a grip on you, the deceit and betrayal begin. Then come the manipulations. The blame. They never take full responsibility. And if they do, it's a half-truth—meant to confuse, to deflect. You're left exhausted and frustrated. You give in.

And just like that, the honeymoon phase returns. The fairy tale is back. Except now, you're carrying unsolved baggage. Since you gave in, it's now yours to hold.

180 DEGREE FAIRY TALE

15

Back to the Beginning Again

A month had passed since I returned to Las Vegas. Edward had purchased tickets months prior for us to see Seal in concert, and despite everything, we went. The concert broke the ice, as he knew it would. And just like that—we were giving our relationship another try.

Nothing about us was ever normal. It was destructive. Twisted. Unlike anything I had ever experienced. Yet somehow, I kept falling back into the cycle. I had learned not to become too attached, though. I knew the next fallout was always just around the corner.

About three weeks later on a Saturday afternoon, sun blazed over Las Vegas, casting sharp shadows across the parking lot. I sat in my car, the engine idling, my phone still connected to Bluetooth. The conversation with Edward had just ended—or so I thought.

"I love you, baby," he had said, his voice warm and reassuring. "I miss you and I can't wait to see you in a few days!", he exclaimed. "Oh! One more thing…I probably won't call you tonight when I get home since it'll be too late. Gotta go, bye!"

I smiled with contentment. I knew this time we'd make it through any challenge going forward.

Then, before I could disconnect the call, I heard a rustling sound and voices come through the speakers.

"Hi, baby." His voice was different now—softer, eager. A faint, feminine voice responding. The sound of a car door closing as she gets into the car. Then the unmistakable sound of a kiss.

"Are you ready?" Edward asked, excitement in his voice. "It's going to be fun tonight!"

My body went rigid. I could feel my heart beating in my head, the adrenaline was racing. My mind raced to make sense of what I was hearing, but the truth was already sinking in, heavy and undeniable.

I should have hung up. I should have spared myself of what came next. But I didn't. I sat there, listening, my whole body was trembling uncontrollably.

And then, like a knife twisting in an already deep wound, I heard my own name.

"So, I'm seeing my attorney on Monday", Edward said, his voice serious with a bit of amusement. "I'll be taking her off my trust and next, I'll be working on getting her out of my house in Vegas." he said in a low calm tone. "I just know she'll destroy it, she's been abusive to me also," he had said in a convincing manner. "It has really taken a toll on me."

Never had I experienced emotions of this magnitude. Every word was a betrayal, every syllable proof that our relationship was nothing more than a lie.

For forty-five agonizing minutes, I listened. Listened as the man I loved unconditionally painted me as a mental tyrant. As he planned a future that no longer included me. As he made her believe she was the only one.

Finally, unable to take another second, I pressed the button and ended the call.

I continued to sit in my car, in a state of confusion, trying to make sense of what just occurred. It was a nightmare, a nightmare in its infancy....

After I gathered myself, I attempted to go into the store, but I was still so disconnected from reality that I walked directly into a grocery cart. I laugh about it now. At the time, I turned around, walked back to my car, and drove straight home. Anger surged through me. I called Edward over and over. I sent texts—long, emotional ones. But I didn't hear from him until the next morning.

He sent an email, which said:

"I am sorry you heard all that last night. I was talking shit. I obviously don't have plans to evict you since I was planning on spending the next 2-3 weeks with you. It was a fabricated story. It was a shitty thing to do and I'm sorry. As for the girl, she is a 29 year old who is friends with an old employee who I met while out a month ago. You and I were broken up at the time, so I invited her to the comedy show. She and I have zero in common being 34 years apart in age. Again, I am so sorry you had to hear all that crap."

He returned to Las Vegas a couple days later and swore she was just a friend. Nothing more had transpired. I didn't believe him. I had zero trust. But I still loved him. I still believed I could fix him.

We had already planned a couple of trips, one of which included attending his family reunion. I decided to go, but right before the event, I got sick. My pancreas flared up again—something I'd experienced before. I knew how to manage it, and the hospital wasn't an option because I knew they'd keep me for days. I hired a mobile nurse who administered two IV bags filled with saline and vitamins. It helped almost immediately.

When Edward returned to the hotel, he was acting cold towards me. He accused me of making an excuse so that I didn't have to be with him and that it was embarrassing to explain my absence.

Once we arrived back home to Las Vegas, I couldn't maintain a facade any longer and act like everything is okay. So, I asked Edward to leave. I had given this man enough of my time, my energy, and sacrificed myself so much that my health was becoming a concern.

Four days later, I received a five-day eviction notice. He had hired a company to process it. They posted the notice on the gate and taped one to the front door. I found a new place two days later and moved in immediately. It was the best thing Edward could have done for me. A few weeks after the eviction, Edward started paying my rent for a few months. I suppose it was his way of easing his guilt.

Fast forward nine months—Edward and I had been more off than on in our situationship. But somehow, we always circled back. At this point, we were finally getting along better than we had in a long time.

And then, just like clockwork, his 29-year-old girlfriend resurfaced. She left him a message saying she was moving to Las Vegas and wanted his advice on what areas to look for a place.

"Perfect timing," I told him. "You'll be retiring soon, spending more time in Vegas. I no longer live in the house—go ahead, move her and her two kids in with you."

"I swear, I haven't seen or talked to her in a year. I barely know her," he replied.

And just when I thought I had seen it all... life said, Not yet.

The next day, I got a text from her and it said, "Give me a call if you want the whole truth.", "I will answer all your questions with 100% honesty...."

I forwarded the texts to Edward before speaking to her wanting to give him the opportunity to explain first out of respect. He didn't answer me.

I called her and we were polite with one another. She began asking me:

"Did you have a male friend of yours call my ex and tell him about Edward and I?", she asked me.

"I have no idea what you're talking about," I replied. "I've never met you. And this ex you're speaking of? I'm confused."

"Maybe it wasn't you. Some guy called my ex and lied about Edward and me. I figured you might've had someone call. Anyway, I want to tell you the truth."

"By all means, go ahead and tell me.", I said. I felt like I was in the Twilight Zone.

Then, she sang like a bird:
"Edward and I met quite awhile ago, I think it was almost two years ago, or a year and a half ago. The second time we met, I went to his condo by the beach. We had mimosas and that's when he asked me to be his girlfriend. He gave me $4000 that day and after that he's been giving me $10,000 a month. He said it's allowance for me and my girls, but he would want to have sex at least three times a week plus pay my bills. He wanted me to spend the night, but I had my 7 year old and my 3 year old with a sitter at home waiting. Not too long ago, he bought me a new Cadillac SUV. I didn't ask him to, he insisted since my other vehicle was a Jeep and it didn't seem safe for my girls

he said. I made sure the Cadillac was in my name because I know he didn't do that for you when he gave you the Corvette. Edward is such a generous man and age has never bothered me, I've always been attracted to older men."

I can remember that conversation like it was yesterday. Halfway through the conversation I felt tense and a sudden heaviness—it was the *energy. Like a*n energetic shift. It was her. She was the dark energy I had been feeling all along. In that moment, I realized it wasn't my imagination. It wasn't anxiety and it wasn't my adrenaline.

It's rare when something like that occurs. But when it does, you don't forget it. It has a distinct nature about it. Ironically, I woke up the following morning with swollen eyes, hives under both of them, and a UTI that had spread to my right kidney. When someone with dark energy disrupts our soul energy, it interferes with our emotions and health and I am certain that was case with my situation

I flew back home the following day. This was one of the most difficult days of my life because I knew that chapter had just come to an end forever and I could never allow myself to return. My journey had to continue moving forward, not stagnated. It was time for me to grow, evolve, and transform into exactly what the Divine spirit intended.

16

The Energy That Shapes Our Lives

Every emotion is a message. A frequency. A whisper from the soul in motion. For most of my life, I didn't know that what I felt wasn't just internal—it was directional. Every fear I carried, every burst of joy, every ache of grief… it wasn't just mine. It was a vibration I was sending into the world.

Energy doesn't lie. It doesn't disappear. It creates. It shapes. It magnetizes. When I held love in my heart, the world opened. When I allowed peace to anchor me, clarity found me.

But when I clung to fear, I only attracted more reasons to stay afraid. Not as punishment—but as confirmation of what I was projecting. What I feel, I emit. What I emit, I receive. And so I began to choose—not perfectly, but consciously.

I chose love, even in uncertainty. I chose gratitude, even in pain. I chose to clear what didn't belong so that what did could return.

I learned that healing isn't just about removing the dark. It's about raising your light. Your vibration is your path. Your emotion is your guide. Your intention is the key. This is how we create our lives: one heartbeat of energy at a time.

And now, I know this for sure: *I am not at the mercy of what happens around me. I am the source of what happens through me.*

The End

17

Understanding Soul Energetic System

In the preceding chapters, I briefly touched on light and dark energy, our soul energetic system and the following I explain in more detail. We often hear things about, the mind, body, and spirit. Ancient healing systems (Ayurveda, Traditional Chinese Medicine, Indigenous medicine) all treat the body and soul as one. But colonization and industrialization pushed those systems aside in favor of clinical science, modern medicine. Spirituality became "personal" instead of "medicinal." While most doctors are trained to avoid anything that can't be proven in a lab or explained in textbooks. And yet, every day, people suffer from illnesses with no clear medical cause—because it might not be physical. Possibly it's energetic.

The Vibration of Happiness (light energy), when you feel genuine happiness— deep, soul-aligned joy—it carries a high frequency that radiates outward from your energetic field. This vibration does several things at once: Your aura expands when you're in a high vibrational state. People around you can feel it, even if they don't consciously recognize it. This is why you'll often notice others feeling calmer, lighter, or more open around you when you're genuinely joyful—because your energy is affecting the field. Our vibration becomes like a beacon, a broadcast of frequency.

It aligns you with similar energy—meaning you begin to attract more experiences, people, and moments that resonate with that frequency. This is where the idea of manifestation comes in: your energy communicates with the field of infinite potential, and the universe responds accordingly. Energy is cyclical. What you send out doesn't just vanish—it returns to you, often in unexpected forms. When your happiness is authentic, it creates a loop—you give light, and light finds its way back. Sometimes through synchronicity. Sometimes through peace. Sometimes through the right person showing up at the right time. In relationships, it's extremely important that both partners operate around the same high vibration, frequency (light energy).

When an unfortunate event occurs in our life, it's normal for our soul energy (chakras) to become off balance or blocked. After a divorce, the heart chakra can become blocked; the adverse effects are emotional disconnection, and a sense of unworthiness or lack of self-love, potentially leading to physical ailments like heart problems or circulatory issues. The throat chakra is about communication, difficulty speaking your truth, feeling unheard, or experiencing physical symptoms like sore throats, thyroid, and neck stiffness. These are just a couple of examples, you'll notice the rest below.

UNDERSTANDING SOUL ENERGETIC SYSTEM

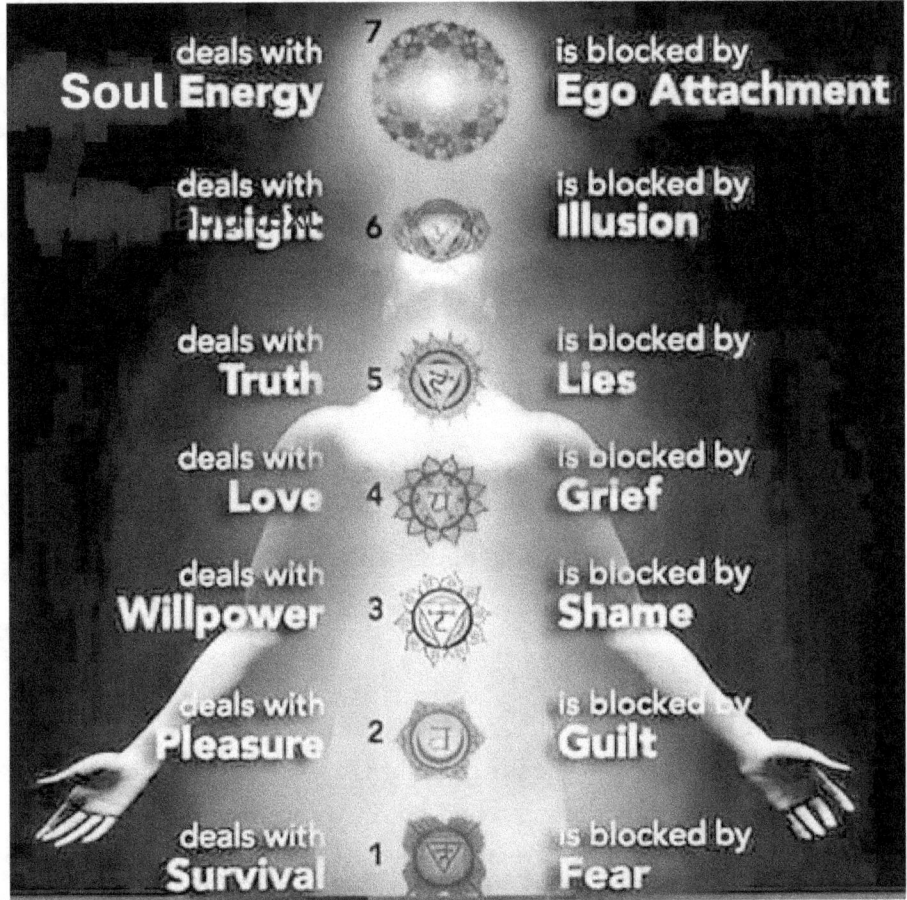

Soul Energetic System (The Chakras) – Transmitters/receivers, communication

- The soul comes from (God, Universe, Higher Self—whatever resonates with your belief system). It's eternal and enters this life with purpose, lessons, and wisdom.
- The soul operates on the emotions of truth, unity, love, expansion etc.
- The chakras are the body's energetic interface between the soul and the physical body.
- Balanced chakras = **Light energy**; enable us to be open to guidance from the Divine, our higher self, spirit strong intuition, feel universal love, and

access spiritual protection.

Repressed Childhood Tramas + Blocked Memory

- When someone experiences childhood traumas, and represses it (often subconsciously), their emotional body stores the trauma, even if their conscious mind doesn't remember.
- The sacral chakra (emotions, sexuality, creativity) and root chakra (safety, trust, survival) are often wounded or blocked.
- The trauma remains "frozen" in the energetic body, leading to:
- Low self-worth
- Shame without a known source
- Chronic low-vibrational states like depression, anxiety, or disconnection
- Memory is blocked, but energy doesn't forget.
- **Dark energy**

The Soul: whispers—with peace, resonance, and alignment.

The soul is understood to operate from the Divine realm—a higher, eternal essence that transcends the mind and body. **Origin:** The soul is said to be a spark of Source (God, Universe, Higher Self—whatever resonates with your belief system). It's eternal and enters this life with purpose, lessons, and wisdom. **Connection to Chakras:** The soul expresses itself through the energy body, particularly via the chakras, which are portals between the **spiritual** and **physical**.

Each chakra can be seen as a channel through which soul energy flows. When balanced, the soul's guidance is more easily received as intuition, inner knowing, love, creativity, and divine connection. **Function:** The soul operates on truth, unity, love, and expansion. It's not attached to image, status, or control—it's here to evolve, to remember its divinity, and to grow through experience.

The Ego: speaks loudest—with fear, doubt, urgency.

The ego operates from the mind and is deeply rooted in our human identity—how we see ourselves, how we want others to see us, and how we navigate survival, success, and social dynamics.

Origin: The ego is a construct of the conscious mind. It's shaped by early childhood experiences, cultural conditioning, societal expectations, and personal achievements or traumas.

Function: Its main goal is protection and separation. It defines "me vs. them" and works to maintain control, certainty, and identity. It often feeds on comparison, judgment, and validation.

Shadow side: When overactive or wounded, the ego can drive fear, insecurity, pride, or defensiveness. It may resist growth because change threatens its sense of identity.

But it's not inherently bad—it's part of being human. A healthy ego allows us to function, set boundaries, and express ourselves confidently without needing to dominate or control.

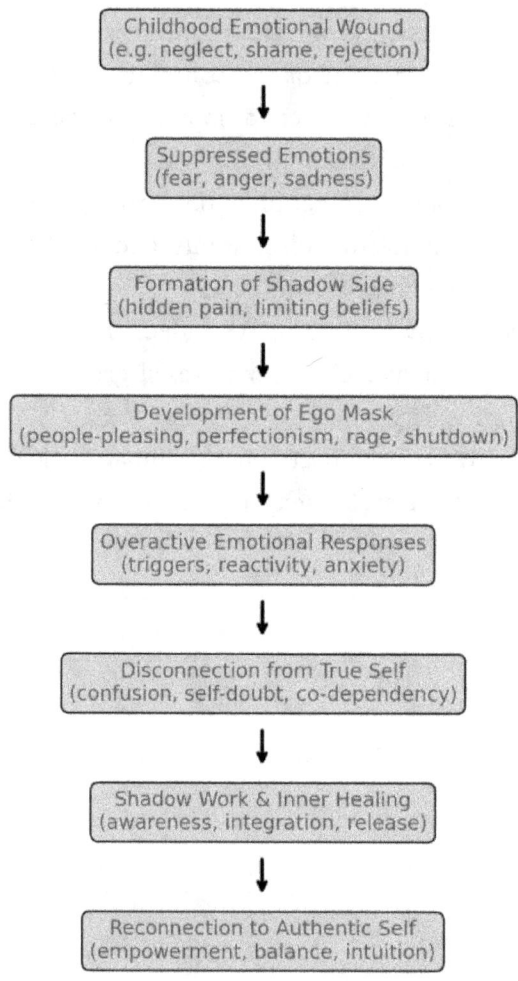

18

Protecting Your Light Energy (High Vibration)

The Vibration of Happiness (Light Energy)

When you feel genuine happiness—deep, soul-aligned joy—it carries a **high frequency** that radiates outward from your energetic field. This vibration does several things at once:

1. It Projects Outward into Your Aura

- Your aura expands when you're in a high vibrational state.
- People around you can **feel it**, even if they don't consciously recognize it.
- This is why you'll often notice others feeling calmer, lighter, or more open around you when you're genuinely joyful—because your energy is affecting the field.

2. It Sends a Signal to the Universe

- Your vibration becomes like a **beacon**, a broadcast of frequency.
- It aligns you with similar energy—meaning you begin to attract more experiences, people, and moments that **resonate** with that frequency.

- This is where the idea of **manifestation** comes in: your energy communicates with the field of infinite potential, and the universe responds accordingly.

3. It Returns to You—Amplified

- Energy is **cyclical**. What you send out doesn't just vanish—it **returns** to you, often in unexpected forms.
- When your happiness is authentic, it creates a loop—**you give light, and light finds its way back.**
- Sometimes through synchronicity. Sometimes through peace. Sometimes through the right person showing up at the right time.

****

Every moment of true happiness contributes to the healing of the collective field. That's the quiet power of a joyful soul—you're not just lighting yourself up, you're lighting the world around you, adding to the collective frequency of love, peace, and light.

You can't truly heal the body if the soul is in pain.
And you can't treat disease without addressing disconnection—from self, from spirit, from purpose.
****

Ways to Take Care of Your Soul Energy

1. **Honor Your Intuition**
2. Your body *always* knows. If something feels off, don't dismiss it. Learn to trust those subtle energetic nudges—they're your soul speaking.
3. **Clear Your Energy Regularly**
4. Use rituals like sage, palo santo, salt baths, sound healing, or visualization

PROTECTING YOUR LIGHT ENERGY (HIGH VIBRATION)

to clear out energetic residue from others. Especially after being around toxic or draining people.

5. **Set Energetic Boundaries**
6. Protect your peace. It's okay to say no. It's okay to walk away. Boundaries are not walls—they're filters for your light.
7. **Limit Access to Your Energy**
8. Not everyone deserves a seat at your table. Be mindful of who you give your time, heart, and presence to. Your energy is sacred.
9. **Connect with Nature**
10. Grounding yourself in nature realigns your frequency. Touch the earth. Feel the sun. Breathe fresh air. Nature is a natural energy cleanser.
11. **Tune into Stillness**
12. Whether it's meditation, deep breathing, or simply sitting in silence, create space for stillness. That's where your soul recharges and reconnects with truth.
13. **Journal to Process & Release**
14. Writing helps you move energy out of the body and onto the page. Let it flow uncensored—tears, rage, hope, all of it.
15. **Call Your Power Back**
16. Say it out loud or write it down: *"I call my energy back from every person, place, and situation that does not serve me."* Your soul hears you.
17. **Surround Yourself with High-Vibration People**
18. Seek those who feel like sunlight—who nourish your soul, not drain it. Energy is contagious, and love without agenda is healing.
19. **Do What Feeds Your Spirit**
20. Dance, paint, cook, laugh, create—whatever makes your soul light up, do more of that. Joy is not a luxury; it's soul maintenance.
21. **Release What Isn't Yours**
22. Empaths often carry other people's emotional weight. Remind yourself: *"This emotion may not be mine. I choose to release it."*
23. **Pray, Speak, or Connect to Source**
24. Whatever your spiritual language—prayer, affirmations, ancestral connection—speak to the divine. Invite protection, clarity, and healing

in.

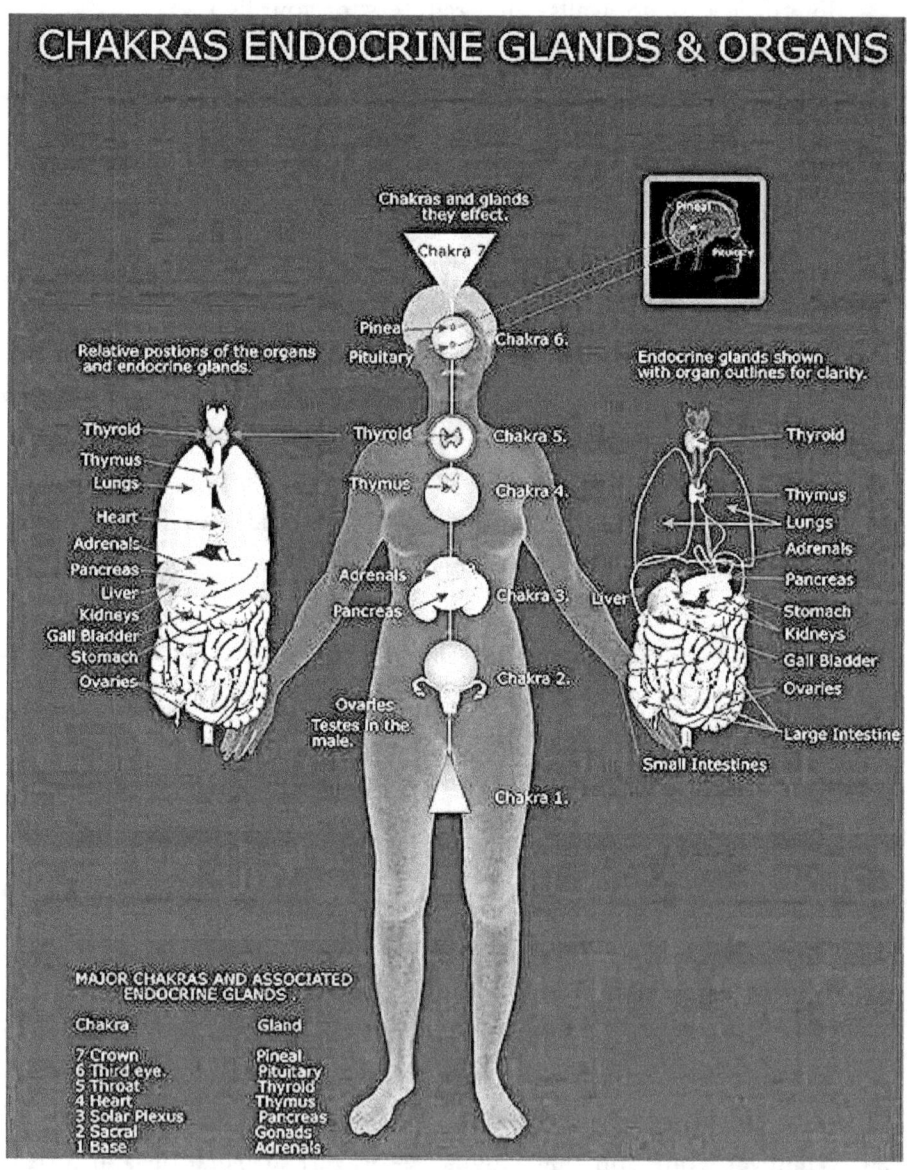

PROTECTING YOUR LIGHT ENERGY (HIGH VIBRATION)

Chakras, Endocrine Glands & Organs – A Spiritual Anatomy Table

Chakra	Color	Location	Endocrine Gland	Organs	Function
Root (Muladhara)	Red	Base of the spine	Adrenal glands	Kidneys, bladder, colon, legs, spine	Safety, survival, grounding, connection to the physical world
Sacral (Svadhisthana)	Orange	Just below the navel	Ovaries / Testes	Reproductive system, pelvic region, lower intestines	Sexual energy, emotions, creativity, relationships
Solar Plexus (Manipura)	Yellow	Upper abdomen	Pancreas	Stomach, liver, gallbladder, digestive organs	Personal power, confidence, self-worth, autonomy
Heart (Anahata)	Green	Center of the chest	Thymus	Heart, lungs, chest, arms	Love, compassion, forgiveness, emotional balance
Throat (Vishuddha)	Blue	Throat	Thyroid / Parathyroid	Throat, neck, jaw, mouth, vocal cords	Communication, truth, expression, integrity
Third Eye (Ajna)	Indigo	Between the eyebrows	Pituitary gland	Eyes, brain, forehead	Intuition, insight, inner wisdom, clarity
Crown (Sahasrara)	Violet / White	Top of the head	Pineal gland	Brain, nervous system	Spiritual connection, divine consciousness, enlightenment

19

My Vision for the World

You can't truly heal the body if the soul is in pain. And you can't treat disease without addressing disconnection—from self, from spirit, from purpose.

Imagine what the world would look like if we normalized spiritual hygiene, energetic checkups, and soul alignment the same way we do physical health. So many illnesses, addictions, breakdowns, and toxic relationships wouldn't just be treated—they'd be understood and healed at the source.

MY VISION FOR THE WORLD

💡 **What That Could Look Like (a future worth dreaming into):**

Soul Wellness Clinics

- Regular energetic checkups (chakra balancing, trauma mapping)
- Grief and soul-fracture recovery
- Guidance through spiritual awakenings or dark nights of the soul

Integrated Medical Teams

- One doctor for the body
- One therapist for the mind
- One soul practitioner for the spirit (energy healer, intuitive, or trauma-informed spiritual counselor)

Preventive Soul Care

- Teach children how to regulate emotions, sense energy, and connect to their inner light
- Normalize journaling, energy work, and breath as sacred practices
- Recognize that spiritual disconnection is as dangerous as malnutrition

Why the Soul Is Overlooked in Western Medicine:

The System Is Rooted in the Physical

- Western medicine evolved from a materialist worldview—what can be seen, touched, measured, or scanned.
- It views the body like a machine: treat the symptom, repair the part.
- But the soul? You can't run a blood test for grief. There's no MRI for a fractured spirit.

The Mind-Body-Spirit Connection Was Separated

- Ancient healing systems (Ayurveda, Traditional Chinese Medicine, Indigenous medicine) all treat the body *and* soul as one.
- But colonization and industrialization pushed those systems aside in favor of clinical science.
- Spirituality became "personal" instead of "medicinal."

Profit & Pharmaceutical Culture

- The current system often treats symptoms to **maintain dependency**, not address the root cause.
- Healing the soul often leads to **true transformation**—which can't be bottled or billed monthly.

Fear of the Unseen

- Most doctors are trained to avoid anything that can't be proven in a lab or explained in textbooks.
- And yet, every day, people suffer from illnesses with no clear medical cause—because it's not physical. It's **energetic**.

20

Conclusion

Boundaries are a clear and deliberate assertion of what we will and will not allow into our life. It is the recognition that our time, our energy and our emotional well-being are finite resources that must be guarded with vigilance. When we fail to establish boundaries, we invite chaos. We allow others to dictate our worth to encroach upon our sense of self to erode our identity, one compromise at a time.

We might find ourselves entangled in relationships that test every part of our being. Relationships with individuals who seem incapable of genuine empathy, who distort reality to suit their own needs and who manipulate as a means of survival. Those with narcissistic tendencies in many ways represents a challenge of the highest order, a force of chaos that enters your life and it wasn't by mere accident. Life was not designed for ease. We are not placed in this world, simply to float along in comfort. Unchallenged, untested growth real meaningful transformation demands hardships. But it also demands we face these hardships head on, so that we might emerge from it stronger, more disciplined, and more aware of our own value.

Hardships are not a mistake, nor is it an unfortunate accident to be avoided. It is in fact the very core in which character is forged, where resilience is tested, and where wisdom is cultivated. Without hardships, there is no growth and without growth, there is no meaning. We can allow it to destroy us, to leave us bitter and broken, or we can allow it to shape us into something greater. This is the central idea of responsibility. We may not have chosen our adversities, but we are responsible for what we do with it. If we learn from it, we become something else entirely, someone who can withstand the storms of life without being torn apart.

Through introspection and reflection, we gain a new perspective of the true nature of life. It is through the wisdom gained from adversity that we navigate life's complexities with clarity and discernment, empowering us to make informed choices and embrace uncertainty with grace.

By embracing challenges as opportunities for growth and transformation, individuals can harness the transformative power of obstacles to shape their destiny and leave a lasting legacy of courage and resilience. As we navigate the twists and turns of life's journey, let us remember that every obstacle is an invitation to grow, evolve, and ultimately, thrive.

Epilogue

Healer's Prayer: A Channel of Light

Divine Source of all healing, light, and love—
　I surrender myself as a vessel for your grace.
　Let your energy flow through me, not from me.
　May my words be guided,
　my presence be pure,
　and my heart remain open.
　I release any need to fix, absorb, or carry.
　I do not own this pain.
　I simply hold space for its transformation.
　May this moment be sacred.
　May this soul be seen.
　And may all healing return to its true origin—
　You.
　So it is.
　And so it shall be.

Affirmation for Alignment:

"*I am a channel of Divine light. I hold space, not burden. I offer presence, not power. I trust the Divine to do what only it can do. I remain protected, guided, and deeply rooted in love.*"

Afterword

www.ingramcontent.com/pod-product-compliance
Lightning Source LLC
Chambersburg PA
CBHW050520100526
44581CB00001B/47